Science-Hobby Book of
# Shell Collecting

# Science-Hobby Book of
# Shell Collecting

**by**
**MIRIAM GILBERT**

ILLUSTRATED BY    HERBERT PIERCE

ISABELLE REID

*Published by*
LERNER PUBLICATIONS COMPANY
Minneapolis, Minnesota

To  KAREN
ANDREA

*and*

KENNETH
PETER
AMY

*and*

LARRY
GARY
RICKY

*and*

*all young seekers of knowledge everywhere, who, I hope,*
*will find a bit of the wonder of the world — through the*
*wonder of a tiny sea shell.*

Second Printing 1971

Revised edition copyright © 1968 by Lerner Publications Company
Original copyright © MCMLXI by Hammond Incorporated

International Standard Book Number: 0-8225-0557-6
Library of Congress Catalog Card Number: 68-54180

Manufactured in the United States of America

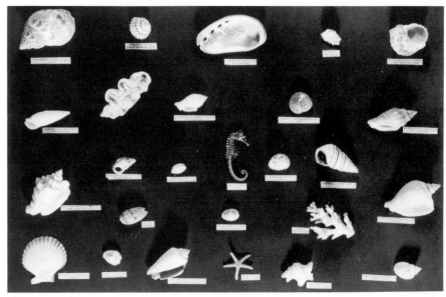

Example of an inexpensive shell collection that may be purchased from the American Museum of Natural History, New York City.

# Foreword

What kind of nature enthusiast are you?

Are you the kind who likes to hike through fields and woods, along streams and lakes to find out about nature first hand? Are you the kind who likes to set up exhibits of live things such as fish and reptiles and growing plants, or to make collections of inanimate things such as rocks and shells and pressed flowers? Or are you possibly the kind who prefers to sit quietly at home reading about nature?

To become a real naturalist you need to be all three kinds.

By getting out into nature you'll see how plants grow, how animals live, and find out how plants and animals depend on each other. By bringing home specimens you'll have a chance to study them at leisure and in close detail. And then, reading about them, you will find out the correct names for what you have seen and collected and will learn what other naturalists have discovered about them.

By going about your nature pursuits in this way, you will pick up a science hobby that will give you hours and days of enjoyment for the rest of your life. But not only that: you will learn to use your eyes to *observe* things, your mind to *figure out* things, and your hands to *do* things — three very important parts of the training of a budding scientist.

WILLIAM HILLCOURT
*Author of* BOY SCOUT HANDBOOK and
FIELD BOOK OF NATURE ACTIVITIES AND CONSERVATION

# CONTENTS

M. Bacheller

# Starting A
# Shell Collection

Did you go to Florida at Christmas and return home with a beautiful conch shell? Is there a shell ornament in your house that your mother has inherited from her mother? Have you walked along the beach or gone clamming in Maine and found a strange looking shell tossed up capriciously out of the ocean which tantalizes you? Shell curiosity can lead to shell collecting.

Shell artistry and artisanship has a long, time-honored history, dating back to the stone-age period. Primitive man, attracted by the delicacy, beauty, shape and color of shells, used them as ornamental decorations — and shells are still popular today for the same reasons.

In the United States many Indian tribes used shells as "wampum," a form of monetary exchange.

During the Victorian era, odd and rare species of shells were actively bought and sold at auctions. They often formed the basis for many valuable collections.

But today shell collecting has entered a new and exciting period, based on a scientific approach. Shell collecting provides a field of widening and rewarding opportunities for the novice. Have you ever held a shell to your ear so you could hear the "sound of the ocean"? With the help of this book, we hope you will learn to use all of your senses — to becomes keenly aware by sight, smell and sound of the many ways in which starting a shell collection may be the start of an exciting scientific hobby for you.

## CLASSIFICATION AND METHOD OF NAMING SHELLS

Just as you should know a person by his "real" name so you should know a shell by its scientific name. These names are usually expressed in Latin so that conchologists all over the world, when exchanging information or consulting about shells, will know, without language barriers, what shell is meant by the proper and precise use of the scientific nomenclature. An orderly, logical plan has been evolved which simplifies the learning of the basic principles used in naming shells.

Scientifically, there are three major classifications of all living matter: Animal, Vegetable and Mineral. Shells are a part of the Animal Kingdom. The Animal Kingdom is further sub-divided into categories, known as *Phyla,* the Greek word for tribe. Each *Phylum* (or single tribe) consists of a group of similar animals that are basically alike.

The name of the *Phylum* to which shells belong is *Phylum Mollusca.* The characteristic that the mollusks have in common is that they all lack a backbone, which means they are invertebrates. In addition, their bodies are soft, as indicated by the derivation of their name from the Latin *mollis* meaning "soft."

THE MOLLUSKS (SHELLS) AND THEIR SUBDIVISIONS

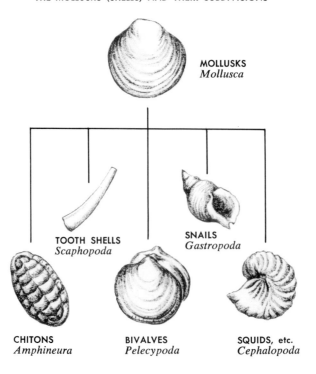

MOLLUSKS
*Mollusca*

TOOTH SHELLS
*Scaphopoda*

SNAILS
*Gastropoda*

CHITONS
*Amphineura*

BIVALVES
*Pelecypoda*

SQUIDS, etc.
*Cephalopoda*

A SNAIL

Lilo Hess, Three Lions, Inc.

The next division below *Phyla* is into classes. Mollusks fall into five classes:

1 — AMPHINEURA — the chitons
2 — SCAPHOPODA — the tooth-shells
3 — CEPHALOPODA — the squids, etc.
4 — PELECYPODA — the clams
5 — GASTROPODA — the snails

Conchologists have further refined the scientific names of shells so that they are highly revealing as to a shell's background, characteristics and origin.

## FIVE CLASSES OF MOLLUSKS

*Phylum Mollusca,* commonly known as "shellfish," makes up one of the largest groups in the Animal Kingdom. It contains approximately 75,000 species. It is also one of the most ancient forms of life on earth. Mollusks have been found in fossil-bearing rocks, which bear credible evidence of their incredible existence more than half a billion years ago!

AMPHINEURA are the lowest forms of mollusks. They have an unusual exterior shell. It is made up of eight separate, saddle-shaped, overlapping plates, held together by a strong girdle made of cartilage. If the girdle is removed, the plates fall apart. The girdle does more than hold the plates together. It gives the chiton protection and maneuverability. It helps flex the chiton's body so it is able to attach itself securely to rough edges or rock; the jointed shell allows it to press into thin crevices in rocks and allows the chiton to curl up into a firm ball when in danger. Its flat, muscular foot is equally specialized for its rock-dwelling, since a pad on it enables the chiton to fasten itself to rocks.

9

SCAPHOPODA, also known as tooth shells or tusk shells because their tube-like shells are shaped like small elephant tusks, make up the smallest class of mollusks.

CEPHALOPODA are the most highly developed mollusks. They include the squid, cuttlefish and octopus which we do not ordinarily think of as "shellfish" and which do not have shells. Only one animal in this class, the chambered nautilus, has an outer shell. Some of the others have an internal shell or "pen."

The picturesque name, *Cephalopoda,* meaning "head-footed" in Greek, describes the many arms, or tentacles, extending from and encircling the head.

PELECYPODA includes the clams, oysters and mussels. The name, which may sound peculiar at first, is based on the Greek word for "hatchet-footed" and calls attention to the odd shape of the single foot.

GASTROPODA is another name derived from the Greek. It means "stomach-footed" and is most apt since this class includes snails, slugs, abalones, whelks, conches and limpets, which move about on their stomachs by means of a large muscular foot.

Most shells fall into the last two groupings, which comprise the largest classes. The *Gastropoda* are univalves, which means the shells are made in one piece. They account for approximately 75% of all shells. The Pelecypoda are bivalves. Their shells are in two parts or "valves," which are hinged together like a door. They constitute about 20% of all shells. The remaining percentage is scattered among the other classes.

ANGEL WING

PEARL OYSTER

## NAMES OF THE MAJOR PARTS OF A UNIVALVE

It is interesting to note the structure of the univalves and the bivalves and to know the proper terminology for the various parts of their bodies and the shells which enclose them.

Pick up a univalve shell and the first thing that usually attracts your attention is the pattern of swirls.

1 — Each complete spiral twist is known as a WHORL. The last and largest whorl is designated the BODY WHORL.

2 — The small whorls at the top are the SPIRE of the shell, just as the spire of a church is on top.

3 — The neighboring edges of two whorls on the spire form a line known as a SUTURE.

4 — Each shell has an APERTURE or opening which is the animal's doorway into the outside world. The aperture, which may be round, oval, semi-circular or elliptical in shape, is also known as the "mouth."

5 — The aperture has an INNER and OUTER LIP, which varies in form and color according to the species. In the majority of shells, the inner lip forms the COLUMELLA which runs through the middle of the shell and basically is the "column" around which the whorls form. The animal is fastened to this support by muscles and thus is able to go in and out of its shell at will.

6 — The OPERCULUM is the safety device which closes off the aperture much like a door being slammed. It is not found in all univalves.

7 — In some univalves, the aperture may have one or two canals: an ANTERIOR CANAL at the lower section of the aperture and possibly a POSTERIOR CANAL, at the upper area of the outer lip. Circular-shaped apertures which lack canals are described as ENTIRE.

The univalve's body is a marvel of complexity and ingenuity. Its head is outfitted with two pairs of tentacles: one pair aids in its sense of feeling, smell and taste; a second, longer pair contains the eyes. The mouth, which is below the tentacles, is amazingly prepared for food-getting. It contains a tongue with teeth! The tongue-shaped structure called the RADULA, which is covered with rows of small, saw-edged teeth on the top surface, is so powerful, it can tear food into bits, and even drill holes through a bivalve shell.

It has a large, flat, muscular foot which can be withdrawn into the shell at the first hint of danger.

The soft bodily structure, protected by its outer MANTLE covering, is even more highly organized than already indicated. Univalves may live in water or on land. Some univalves have lung-like air sacs, which makes it possible for them to get oxygen directly from the air. Others have a single gill, hiden within the MANTLE CAVITY, which is the area between the mantle and the body. Still others have both the air sacs and the gills.

The univalve is equipped with a MANTLE by which it builds its shell. The mantle secretes a lime solution which hardens as it comes in contact with the air and forms the SHELL. In time, as the shell becomes too cramped

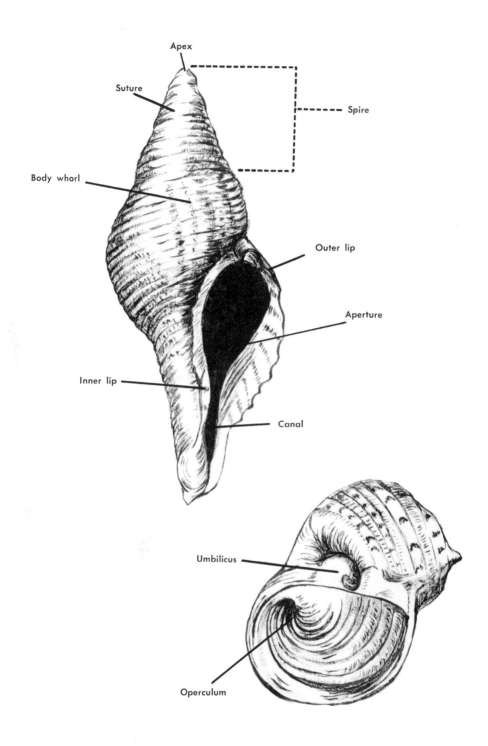

Apex

Suture

Spire

Body whorl

Outer lip

Aperture

Inner lip

Canal

Umbilicus

Operculum

UNIVALVE SHELLS

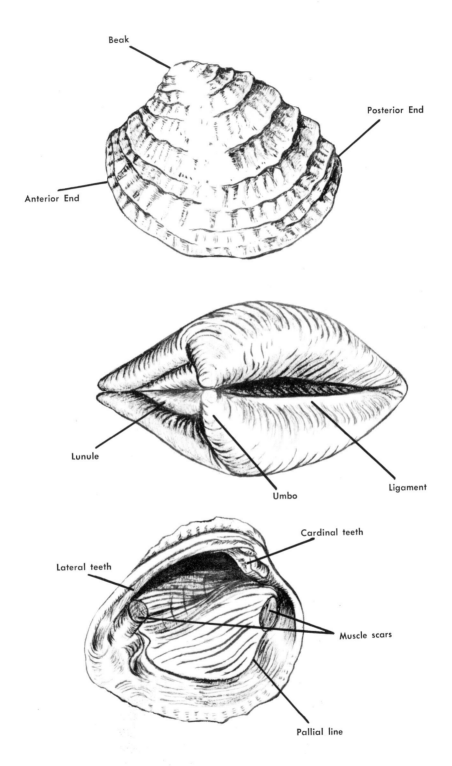

Beak

Posterior End

Anterior End

Lunule

Umbo

Ligament

Cardinal teeth

Lateral teeth

Muscle scars

Pallial line

BIVALVE SHELLS

for the animal, it builds a new addition. This pattern and process of growth is amazing in its adaptability. It is not a steady process but is broken by inactive periods. As a result of this fluctuation in shell secretion, growth lines are earmarked on the shell.

Univalve shells vary in color. This variation is caused by pigment glands found along the margin of the mantle. They also vary in hardness: some are hard and shiny, others are crumbly and chalky. Most univalve shells are right-handed, like most people — with the spiral whorls twisting to the right. In some species, the shell spirals turn to the left. These are called left-handed shells. Occasionally, a right-handed shell turns to the left. Such oddities are called "sports." To guide you in recognizing a right-handed from a left-handed shell, hold the shell with the spire pointing up; then the aperture should be on the right. If you are observing a live univalve as it advances forward, the point of the shell, the APEX, faces in the opposite direction.

## NAMES OF THE MAJOR PARTS OF A BIVALVE

In a bivalve, the two shells or "VALVES" are gripped by interlocking TEETH and a LIGAMENT. There is a "left" and a "right" valve. The front of the shell is called the ANTERIOR, the back — POSTERIOR. The hinged portion of the shell is raised and is called the UMBO or BEAK because of the beak-like shape. In some bivalves, in front of the umbo, there is a distinctive heart-shaped depression known as the LUNULE.

It is interesting to compare and contrast the bivalves and univalves. The bivalve moves about in the same fashion as the univalve, using its one thick FOOT to inch it forward. The bivalve has no distinct head, tentacles or well-developed sensory organs as does the univalve. It breathes through gills, which take up a large part of the mantle cavity.

To compensate for these deficiencies, some bivalves depend on a pair of elongated SIPHONS for water, air and food. A system is set up whereby water is sucked into one of the siphons, bringing with it oxygen and bits of food. This water is then passed off, through the other siphon, carrying waste products, which are disposed of through the shell. The siphons are flexible enough to reach far out of the shell and the animal may be hidden in sand or mud and still get food and air.

A bivalve can't conceal its age. The shell shows the same growth lines as in the univalve, layer upon layer formed from calcium carbonate.

PEARLY OYSTER

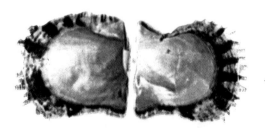

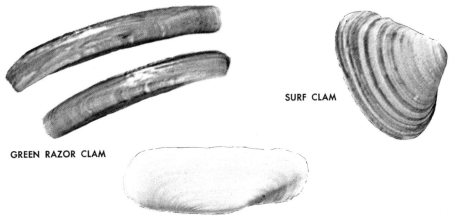

GREEN RAZOR CLAM

SURF CLAM

STOUT RAZOR CLAM

Also, as in the case of the univalve, the mantle is highly important. In the bivalve, the mantle is a thin membrane which lines the shell and performs more functions than that of protecting the soft body of the animal and secreting the material that forms the shell. To some degree, it acts as a sensory organ since in some species, nerve cells, highly responsive to light and touch, run along the rim of the mantle. The iridescent lining on the inside of the shells of some oysters, mussels and similar shells is due to the deposit of nacreous material between the layers.

## FAMILIAR BIVALVES

You may be confronted with such a bewilderingly beautiful array and display of shells, depending on the region where you do your collecting, that it may be difficult to know where to begin and what to gather. One good way to learn about something unfamiliar is to lead off with the familiar. Most of us are familiar with the edible varieties of clams, oysters, scallops and mussels, and so let's start with these bivalves.

## SOME COMMON CLAMS

QUAHOG *Mercenaria mercenaria,* — "round," "littleneck," "hard-shelled" and "cherrystone," these are just a few of the names by which this clam is known. It is found from Canada to Florida, and commercially it is the most important clam on the east coast. Historically, it was made into beads, called wampum, by the Indians, and used for money, which explains the derivation of the name *mercenaria.* Visually, its interior white shell, edged with a purple border, was considered so beautiful that in former times it was known as *Venus Mercenaria.*

GREEN RAZOR CLAM *Solen viridis,* also has a beautiful shell. It is quite small, usually no more than two or three inches in length, but it has a pretty pale green color, with a smooth, glossy surface. Its odd shape, reminiscent of the short old-fashioned razors, makes it easily identifiable. It is scattered along the eastern coast from southern New England to Florida but is most prevalent in the southern area. If you chance upon one, you will probably find more since they generally group together in colonies.

STOUT RAZOR CLAM *Tagelus gibbus,* is another shell which may be recognized by its oblong shape. It is white or yellowish, grows to about four inches, and your best chances of finding it are in muddy areas from New England southward since it is a mud-burrower.

SURF CLAM *Spisula solidissima,* found in the surf from Labrador to North Carolina,is the largest bivalve along the north Atlantic coast. It is six inches in length, yellowish white in color and has a thick, triangle-shaped shell. At a New England clam bake, this is the clam you find often used.

OYSTERS (Commercial and Precious Varieties):

VIRGINIA OYSTER *Ostrea virginica,* the common oyster, found from Maine to Florida, does not produce pearls of gem quality, does not flaunt a pearly lining, but it does rank as No. 1 in commercial value among shellfish.

THE PEARL OYSTER known generically as *Pinctada,* produces the pearls of precious value. Some pearl oysters produce more pearls than others. The leading pearl producer in the family is the *Pinctada vulgaris,* found mainly in the Persian Gulf and the Gulf of Mannar, India.

THE GREAT PEARL OYSTER *Pinctada maxima,* found in Ceylon and the Persian Gulf, and off the northern coast of Australia, produces the largest pearls, some as magnificent as twelve inches in size. It is valued equally for the lustrous layer of mother-of-pearl on the inside of its shell. The mother-of-pearl consists of liquid nacre which has hardened and formed in flat layers, and is the same secretion that makes the pearl. The pearl oyster family is found in many parts of the world and species in different warm waters produce pearls that vary amazingly, running the color gamut from white to black, with shadings of pink, yellow, gray, and brown in between.

Nature has endowed the oyster with the gift of making pearls as a protective device. If a bit of foreign matter, such as a grain of sand or a parasite, becomes stuck in the mantle of the oyster, the mollusk secretes a liquid to cover the irritating object. This is the beginning of a pearl. As more and more of the liquid nacre is added, the pearl grows in size. In the early 1900's, Kokichi Mikimoto, a Japanese, discovered a method of inducing the artificial formation of pearls, which has resulted in the cultured pearl industry.

SPINY TREE OYSTER *Pinctada radiata* The exterior of this shell is rough yet the lining is so iridescent it is often called the "Pearly Oyster." The average length is approximately two inches, color is variable, usually a greenish brown and the shell is found on both coasts of Florida.

SCALLOPS (Jet-propelled Pelecypods)

The scallop *(Pecten),* has a highly scientific built-in method of locomotion. It advances through the water in sudden spurts by rapidly opening and closing its valves. The motor power is furnished by a large muscle, the edible part of the scallop, which controls the closing of the shells. Two streams of water, forced out through openings in the mantle by the snapping of the shells together, propel the scallop along. Another unusual feature of the pectens is a row of tiny, bright eyes which rings the edge of the mantle.

PECTEN NODOSUS

TEREBRATALIA
OCCIDENTALIS

VENUS MERCENARIA

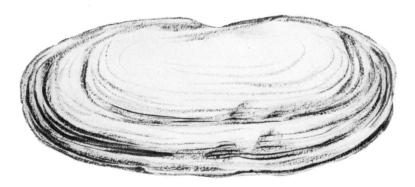

FLAT RAZOR CLAM

PECTEN LAQUEATUS

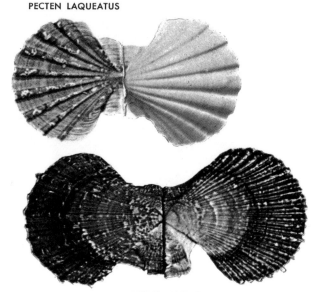

PECTEN NOBILIS

PECTEN LAETUS

The adults swim about freely but the young are fastened by a byssus to a firm object. Basically, a byssus is a self-made anchor. It is made of tough threads, formed from a sticky, fast-hardening substance, which secures the bivalve to a steady support.

Helpful identifying features include: circular shells and small wings or ears which protrude on either side of the hinge of the shell. Scallops are found on both the Atlantic and Pacific coasts of the United States.

BAY SCALLOP *Pecten irradians* is the common scallop on the eastern seaboard ranging from New England to North Carolina.

CALICO SCALLOP *Pecten gibbus* is another common species but is found further south, from North Carolina to Cuba. Because of its bright and varied colors (mottled white, rose, brown and purple) and its size, one to one and a half inches, it is highly popular for shell novelties.

DEEP-SEA OR GIANT SCALLOP *Pecten grandis,* the largest American scallop, measures six to seven inches across. It favors deep water, ranging from Newfoundland to New Jersey. The upper valves, which are slightly convex, were used by the Indians as dishes. Today souvenir hunters have adapted them for modern usage as ash trays.

LION'S-PAW *Pecten nodosus* This is a collector's prize. Just as rarity makes gems precious so rarity makes this shell precious. It is not usually found on beaches. It lives in deep water from North Carolina to the Florida coast and is sometimes found by sponge fishermen. It is a vividly colored shell: the interior is shiny and pink; the outer part varies from red to bright orange. The sculptured lion's paw effect is created by radiating ribs and raised knobs on the surface. This shell is from four to six inches in diameter. Other magnificent pectens found in Pacific waters are: *Pecten nobilis, Pecten laqueatus, Pecten lætus.*

18

## MUSSELS

BLUE MUSSEL *Mytilus edulis* is the common, blue-black species, approximately three inches in length, found along the Atlantic coast. It attaches itself to rocks in the same manner as the young scallop, by weaving a byssus. Mussels are also widespread in rocky areas along the Pacific coast.

CALIFORNIA MUSSEL *Mytilus californianus* is larger than the eastern species. It may grow up to eight inches in size. It has a shiny, purplish-black shell, which is sometimes streaked with brown. The Indians discovered these shells could be filed to needle sharpness and used them as harpoons in fishing.

As soon as you have made some headway in gathering a general collection of shells, you will begin to specialize. You may decide to group your shells according to the region where you found them; or separate them scientifically into the five classes of mollusks; or you may even concentrate on building up a single genus of shells. You may also center your collection around the shape, color, or idiosyncracies of some of the species and unusual characteristics of the shells. Let's consider some shells from the vantage points of this breakdown:

### SHELLS WITH DESCRIPTIVE NAMES AND DISTINCTIVE SHAPES

What's in a name? A great deal when it comes to the names of shells. They often are so accurately and aptly named that it is a vivid give-away as to one or more of a shell's peculiarities.

STAR SHELL *Astræa longispina* You could almost guess that this would be star-shaped with long spines. It is approximately two inches across, has a silvery iridescence and is found in southern Florida where it is made into shell jewelry and souvenirs.

TURRET SHELL *Turritella exoleta* Delicate swirls of white and brown entwine this slender shell, culminating in a long spire and a pointed apex. It grows to a height of about three inches and is found in southern Florida and the West Indies.

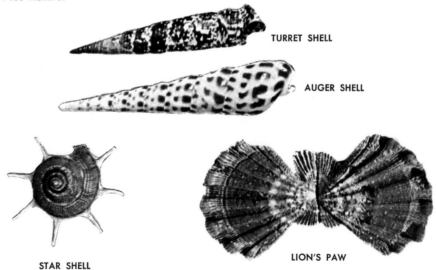

TURRET SHELL

AUGER SHELL

STAR SHELL

LION'S PAW

Collection of univalve and bivalve shells                                B. Amlick

AUGER SHELL *Terebra goniostoma,* ashy gray to pale brown in color, about two inches in size, is another gracefully elongated shell which rises to a fine point. It is found extensively in Florida but ranges from Virginia to Texas.

NORTHERN DIPPER SHELL *Cuspidaria glacialis,* is a good example of the special characteristic of the "dipper shells." It is a small (about three-fourths of an inch), grayish-white, pear-shaped bivalve with its posterior end tapering off to a handle-like formation. It prefers fairly deep water and is found as far north as Canada and as far south as Florida.

SPOON SHELL *Periploma leanum,* is another small (about an inch in length), white shell with a particularized feature. It has a spoon-shaped "tooth" in each valve. It is found in shallow water all the way from the Gulf of St. Lawrence to North Carolina.

BLEEDING TOOTH *Nerita peloronta,* has not one tooth but very often two teeth to distinguish it. These are gleaming white protrusions on the inner lip, which stand out strongly because the rest of the columellar margin is yellowish-orange. It is a small (one to one and a half inches in diameter), globe-shaped shell found from Florida to the West Indies.

TAPESTRY SHELL *Turbo petholatus,* is a top-shaped shell found in tropical waters. The operculum is so strikingly beautiful that it is used in many islands of the South Pacific for jewelry.

KNOBBY TOP SHELL *Turbo castaneus,* is sometimes called the "chestnut top

Unusual Marine shells

B. Amlick

shell" because of its brownish color. The shell is round in shape like a top, with the apex rising to a sharp point. It is a pretty shell, ornamented with several whorls of beads. It prefers shallow water and a mild temperature, being found from North Carolina to Mexico.

PYRAMID OR OBELISK SHELL *Pyramidella dolabrata,* is a small (one inch), delicately pale yellow shell, with a tiny surface. The shell tapers off to a sharp point like a pyramid.

WEST INDIAN WORM SHELL *Vermicularia spirata-philippi,* can't be surpassed when it comes to shell oddities. Its erratic twisted shape hardly seems natural. It is predominately yellow in color and often marked with brown. It may be found in fairly shallow water, from North Carolina to the West Indies.

SCORPION SHELL *Pterocera scorpio,* is another uniquely shaped shell. The lips are wide and edged with long spines that give the shell the appearance of a spider or scorpion. Just as nature can create bizarre shell fantasies, it can also create shell beauties.

HARP SHELL *Harpa crenata,* is an example of a beautifully shaped shell, but this is the only one of its species in American waters. The small miter shells are distinctively shaped shells. They are recognized by their spindle shape and a sharply pointed spire.

KNOBBY MITER *Mitra nodulosa,* which is about 2 inches high and pale brown in color is found from North Carolina to the West Indies. Larger species are found in the Pacific and Indian oceans.

SPOON SHELL

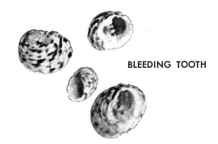

BLEEDING TOOTH

## SEA PENS

Sea pens also have large shells, measuring more than a foot long, but in contrast to the tritons, the shells are fragile and easily broken.

FLESH SEA PEN *Pinna carnea,* is a pale orange-yellow species, found from North Carolina to the West Indies. It is secured by a silky but amazingly powerful byssus.

SAW-TOOTHED SEA PEN *Atrina serrata,* is found in the same general area as the stiff sea pen. It is brown to brownish black and has the same pie-wedge shape as the stiff sea pen, but is larger and more delicately sculptured.

STIFF SEA PEN *Atrina rigida,* has a thin, triangular amber-colored shell which clearly shows its similarity in shape to the quill pen, from which it derives its name. The valves are adorned by some 15 raised and spiny ribs particularly along their outer margin. It also attaches itself by a byssus to some support, which it definitely needs since it lives in deep water, where it is constantly buffeted about. It covers a wide range from North Carolina to South America.

Here are some shells that sound as if they belonged in a zoo: tusk shells which belong to the class Scaphopoda. ELEPHANT'S TOOTH *Dentalium elephantinum,* a tube-like shell, usually ivory-white in color, is open at both ends and so it was easy to string and use as ornaments. The West Coast Indians also used tusk shells for money. It was called Dentalium Shell money. One species gained such popularity, it was called PRECIOUS TUSK SHELL *Dentalium pretiosum.*

TAPESTRY SHELL

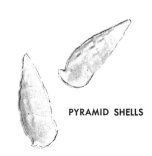

PYRAMID SHELLS

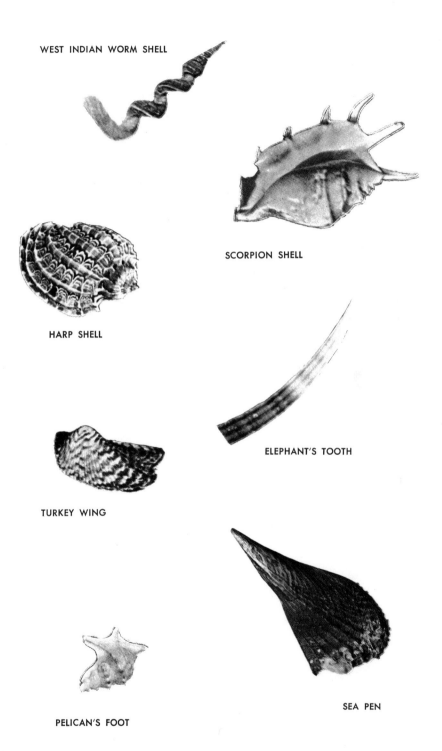

WEST INDIAN WORM SHELL

SCORPION SHELL

HARP SHELL

ELEPHANT'S TOOTH

TURKEY WING

SEA PEN

PELICAN'S FOOT

TURKEY WING *Arca occidentalis,* is a colorful name for a colorful clam. The oblong shell which has a winged appearance is open at both ends. It is yellowish white, with reddish-brown stripes on the outside, while the interior is a lovely shade of lavender. The length is two to four inches. It hides in rock crevices, anchored by a byssus, and is seen frequently on southern beaches from North Carolina to Cuba.

In this same *Arcidæ family, Genus Arca,* the BLOODY CLAM or BLOOD ARK *Arca pexata,* is a very interesting species. It is one of the rare mollusks with red blood. Usually mollusks have light pink blood. It has a thick white shell, is about two inches long and may be found along the eastern coastline from Maine to Florida.

PELICAN'S FOOT *Aporrhais pes-pelicani,* is a European shell, sought after because of its odd shape. In this shell the lip, which juts out beyond the body of the shell, has three tapering pointed spines, which look like the toes on a pelican's foot.

Not to be outdone, the United States has the DUCK FOOT *Aporrhais occidentalis.* It has a thick grayish white shell, about two inches high, uniquely marked with folds resembling half-moons. The outer lip flares out into a wide, wing-like expanse, which makes this shell easily recognizable. It is a deep water species, ranging northward from North Carolina to Labrador.

TRITONS (Spectacular Musical Shells)

Tritons have been fashioned into shell trumpets from time immemorial. These shells were named in honor of Triton, a mythological Greek demigod of the seas. He is usually depicted as blowing on a trumpet shell, with which he can magically stir up or soothe the waters of the sea. The trumpets are made by cutting a hole in the spire of the shell. The species found in the United States belong to the Family *Cymatiidæ.*

HAIRY TRITON *Cymatium aquitile,* measures about 4-6 inches and is usually a light brown, with bands of gray and white. It is found in southern Florida, the West Indies and also in the Pacific.

RIBBED TRITON *Cymatium cynocephalum,* is a smaller triton (about three inches), pale yellow in color, with occasional gray and white shadings. The surface is dominated by horizontal or revolving ribs, which are easily identifiable. It is found in the Florida Keys, on the Gulf Coast of Texas and in the West Indies.

OREGON TRITON *Argobuccinum oregonensis,* is a Pacific Coast species found from Alaska to Monterey, California. It has a hairy brown covering which contrasts with the clear-white interior. It grows to a length of about four inches.

TRITON'S TRUMPET *Charonia tritonis,* the king of all tritons, is also known as trumpet shell. Its size would be noteworthy in itself since it grows as long as eighteen inches. But, in addition, it is vividly colored in crescentic designs of buff, brown, purple and red. This species is found in the Indian Ocean, the Philippines and in Japan, where it has been used by Shinto priests for many centuries to summon the people to religious services.

BLACK KATY

OREGON TRITON

CHITONS (The Animal With The Suit Of Armor)

The chitons are like the limpets in some ways. They fasten themselves to rocks in a similar fashion and they are also protectively colored brown, gray or black to obscure themselves on the rocks on which they live. But this mollusk is like no other since it has an unusual set of eight overlapping shells to protect itself, which has earned it the nickname "coat-of-mail shells." They are most common on the west coast of the United States since they prefer warm waters.

BLACK KATY *Katharina tunicata,* is found from Oregon to Catalina, California. The overlapping plates are black and the vacuum disk foot reddish. The way this small two to three inch chiton got its big name is interesting. "Katy in a tunic" refers to Lady Katharine Douglas who is credited with having sent the first specimen of the species to the British Museum.

EASTERN CHITON *Chætopleura apiculata,* one-third to three-fourths inches long is found in shallow water from Cape Cod to Florida.

WEST INDIAN CHITON *Chiton tuberculatus,* approximately one inch long, is abundant in the West Indies.

# LIMPETS

There are two groups of limpets: one has shells that are entire; the other, known as the keyhole limpet, has a keyhole shaped opening in the top part of the shell.

The limpet has no operculum and so nature compensates by providing other means of protection. The limpet is able to pull its shell tightly over its body. The limpet's foot provides more than a method of locomotion. It acts like a clamp and helps to keep it fastened to a rock. The limpet can anchor itself so firmly to a support that it is sometimes impossible to pry one free without breaking the shell. Most species are protectively colored and blend so well with the rocks or seaweed to which they attach themselves that they are easily overlooked.

LITTLE KEYHOLE LIMPET *Diodora cayenensis,* about one to two inches in length, has the distinctive keyhole slit. It is usually white but occurs in a variable color range. It may be pink, buff or deep gray. It is found from Maryland to Brazil.

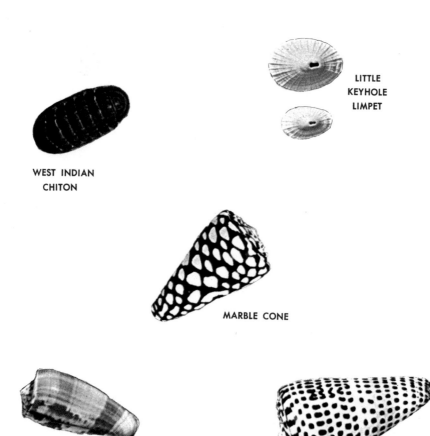

LITTLE
KEYHOLE
LIMPET

WEST INDIAN
CHITON

MARBLE CONE

STRIATE CONE

LETTERED CONE

CONES

M. Bacheller

CONES

## COWRIES

The cowry is so timid, it hides within its own mantle! The mantle extends on each side, forming two lobes, which the cowry can fold over, almost covering the entire back of the shell. This helps to protect the cowry's shell and explains why the outer shell is so smooth and glossy.

The young cowry begins life with a spiral shell much like the shells of other snails. As the cowry matures, it loses its spiral shape and becomes more oval in contour. Another sign of maturity is a slitlike aperture, which is edged with teeth on both the inner and outer lips.

Most cowries are tropical shells and are found widely throughout Africa and the South Pacific, where they were used at one time as money. One species of cowry was used as money for so long, it was called the MONEY COWRY *Cypræa moneta.*

MEASLED OR SPOTTED COWRY *Cypræa exanthema,* also sometimes known as *Cypræa zebra,* is an American species found from North Carolina on southward. It is three to four inches long, a purplish brown, with round white dots sprinkled over it, which give it its name.

RING TOP COWRY

MONEY COWRY

STRIPED CONE

## ECCENTRICS AMONG THE SHELLS (Shells With Idiosyncracies)

Cone shells are so breathtakingly beautiful and occur in so many brilliantly patterned species, they can be included under the "color" group. Since they eat fish, crabs and even their own kind, they can also be classified under the "carnivorous species." But a large group of cones possess one unique trait — they are deadly!

Many cones found in the tropical waters of the Indian and South Pacific oceans possess a gland at the back of the head which produces a venom. In launching an attack on its prey, the cone extends its long, tubular proboscis, releases a poison through it, to pierce its enemies. There have been verified reports that a cone can kill an octopus and in some instances, the poison has been known to prove fatal to humans. Cones occur in the United States from the Carolinas to Florida but are of the harmless species.

MARBLE CONE *Conus marmoreus,* a poisonous species, is a cone with a solid white shell so heavily patterned in black that it creates the opposite illusion of being a black shell with white spots. The LETTERED CONE *Conus litteratus* is another example of a solid cone, artistically sprayed with such a profusion of dots and dashes that it looks like a jumble of letters.

CHINESE ALPHABET CONE *Conus spurius atlanticus,* is an outstandingly beautiful cone found on both the eastern and western coasts of Florida. It is the largest cone found on the Atlantic coast, reaching from two to three inches in height. Its smooth shell is unmistakably shaped like an inverted cone. It is creamy white, set off with spiral rows of orange and brown spots, which sometimes look like the letters of the alphabet.

CARRIER SHELL *Xenophora trochiformis,* is a garbage collector! As it grows it gathers odds and ends of coral, tiny bivalve shells and small pebbles which it attaches to the top of its own shell. These particles are so skillfully placed that they follow the suture line, forming a spiral. As the carrier shell matures, it keeps piling on more and larger pieces. This apparent bit of madness is a protective camouflage since the alien fragments cloak the carrier shell from potential enemies.

This strange yellowish brown univalve is two inches in diameter, round and top-shaped, and is found from North Carolina to Cuba carrying its own self-made burden.

**CHAMBERED NAUTILUS**

CHAMBERED NAUTILUS *Nautilus pompilius*, the apartment house mollusk, builds a new room for itself every time it grows and needs larger quarters. By the time the chambered nautilus is mature, it has left behind it in its spiral shell a series of chambers, graduated larger and larger in size.

This amazing process of growth and expansion which results in an apartment house shell made up of many "chambers" takes place in the following way: The chambered nautilus, when young, has only one chamber. As it grows, it moves forward where there is more room. It then seals off the old "chamber" with secretions from its mantle. The inside of the chambers are lined with mother-of-pearl. The outside of the shell is yellowish white with brown spiral bands. It is found in the South Pacific and the Indian Ocean.

ANGEL'S WING *Barnea costata* These snow-white shells, six to seven inches in length, with the angelic look and name, have a devilish habit of being able to bore holes in wood, coral and fairly hard rock.

The shells are surprisingly thin and brittle, apparently unsuited for such painstaking labor. They are rough, however, with strong ribs giving a spiny surface on the outer edges, and by patient, steady twisting, turning and rubbing, the angel's wing can grind off a large enough space in a rock in which to live. With this kind of family background, it is no wonder that the angel's wing is a mud and sand burrower and may dig down as deep as one foot. The angel's wing is a species which is most common in Florida but it ranges from Cape Cod to the West Indies.

## THE FIGHTERS (The Carnivorous Species)

Conch shells include a widespread group of beautiful but beastly-mannered, warm-water, carnivorous snails.

QUEEN CONCH *Strombus gigas,* is one of the largest and heaviest gastropods. It reaches between eight to twelve inches and weighs up to five pounds. Its shell is creamy yellow on the outside and a delicate rose-pink on the inside. It ranges from Northern Florida to the West Indies. It feeds upon dead animal food but will also attack living bivalves.

CROWNED CONCH *Melongena Corona,* found on both the east and west coasts of Florida, is adorned with sharp spines which cover the large body whorl and several of the whorls of the short spire. It has a shiny shell, two to five inches in height, ringed with brown stripes.

FIGHTING CONCH *Strombus pugilis,* puts up a big fight for a little fellow (three to five inches in height). The shell, common in the West Indies, is large and solid. The outside is plain yellowish brown but the inside of the aperture is vividly colored in orange or purple.

FLORIDA CONCH *Strombus alatus,* is closely related as far as pugnacity is concerned. It is about the same height as the fighting conch and also is yellowish brown, but may sometimes be striped with orange and purple.

MUREX                                                    M. Bacheller

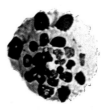

CARRIER SHELL

CROWNED CONCH

MUREX PELE

LINED WENTLETRAP *Epitonium lineatum,* is another predatory, carnivorous snail. They are sometimes called "staircase shells" because the shells are high spired, with many whorls. They are rarely found by the average collector since they are small (one-half inch high) and creep about on the ocean floor at great depths. Their habitat covers the Atlantic coast from Massachusetts to Florida.

LADDER SHELL *Epitonium groenlandicum* This wentletrap displays the characteristic tapering shell which culminates in a point. It is found off the Maine coast and is essentially a cold water species. It averages an inch in height and is white or yellowish brown in color.

## MUREX SHELLS

The murex was known and valued in ancient times for its dye-producing fluid, which is secreted by a gland in the inner wall of the mantle of the murex. The dye, named "Tyrian purple" after the city of Tyre which was famous for its dye-making, was used to dye the robes of royalty and is the origin of the term "royal purple."

APPLE MUREX *Murex pomum,* is a predatory species, totally unaware of royal manners. It is a little beauty, however, one and a half to two inches in size, yellowish white, with wide stripes and flecks of brown, set off by a rose colored aperture. The shell which is rough-textured and heavy may be identified by three spiny varices, running lengthwise across the whorls. The species ranges widely from North Carolina to Venezuela.

BLACK LACE MUREX *Murex florifer,* bears its own stamp of nobility. It is a "fancy" shell, brownish black in color, with a pink aperture and containing approximately seven whorls that are embellished with leaflike spines. It is about one to two inches in height and a familiar shell on beaches ranging from North Carolina to South America.

LINED WENTLETRAP

LADDER SHELL

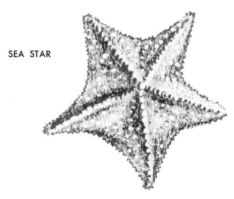

SEA STAR

SCOTCH BONNET

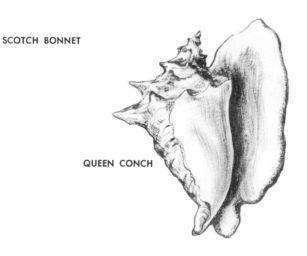

QUEEN CONCH

## HELMET SHELLS

These belligerent univalves have a large, heavy shell, with a thickened outer lip, which is used in making cameos.

YELLOW HELMET *Cassis madagascarensis* This is the "giant" in the species, reaching a length of about ten inches. It is a faded yellow color, with a prominent outer lip, ridged with large teeth, and the inner lip lined with smaller teeth. It lives in shallow water, from North Carolina to the West Indies.

SCOTCH BONNET *Phalium granulatum* This "helmet" carries some of the family traits. It is creamy yellow in coloration; the shell is three to four inches in length; is heavy and the outer lip is thickened and lined with teeth. The distinctive feature of this snail is the light-brown squares set in a definite pattern over the shell. It is an aggressive species, attacking bivalves, which it digs up by burrowing in the mud. It is found from North Carolina southward.

## MOON SHELLS

These snails, delicately rounded in contour, with their well-defined half-moon shaped aperture, are vicious carnivores. They stamp their enemies to death! The moon snail has an enormous foot, which it uses to hold fast its prey, while it then proceeds to bore a hole through the shell of the hapless victim with its coarse tongue.

CAT'S EYE *Natica maroccan* This snail has earned the name "cat's eye" because of its button-like top. For a small (about one and a half inches) creature, it has gained a big reputation as a predacious species. It is found from North Carolina to Florida and must be looked for carefully since it is brown in color and often hidden, burrowing beneath the mud.

COMMON NORTHERN MOON SHELL *Polinices heros,* is found scattered abundantly on beaches from Maine to New Jersey. It has a large, distinctively oval aperture, is ashy brown in color and averages about four inches in height.

TULIP SHELL *Fasciolaria tulipa* A large (four to six inches in height), lazy, carnivorous species, deplored as a conch killer because of its predilection for the pink conch. It is beautifully shaped with an elevated spire and a sharp point and is equally attractive color-wise with its pinkish gray shell, adorned with spirals of dark brown. It ranges from North Carolina, along the Gulf Coast states to Texas.

BANDED TULIP SHELL *Fasciolaria distans,* a smaller species (three inches in height), bluish-gray in color, with brown spiraling lines, also boasts a shapely spindle-contour. It is quite common along the Florida shoreline but occurs from North Carolina to Texas.

## ARTISTIC SHELLS (Noted For Their Colors And Patterns)

LAND SNAILS — These are snails that have lungs. Most land snails have shells and some of the shells are so spectacularly colored it is almost impossible to believe that they are natural and not painted.

Cuba is noted for its many species of land snails some of which make their home in trees, and thus are sometimes called Cuban tree snails. The infinite multiplicity of color and grouping of colors of these snails is breathtaking: yellow circled with red, brown with white bands, blue trimmed with white, red, sharply banded with black and white; these are only a few of the combinations in which they occur. The PAINTED SNAILS *Polymita picta,* shown on page 35, are found only in Oriente Province, Cuba. Some species are so beautiful that they are highly sought after. Florida, also, has several species of land snails. However, some, such as the beautiful tree snails *(Liguus),* are rapidly becoming extinct.

LETTERED OLIVE *Oliva sayana* If you come across an olive that is alive, you can usually depend on finding a colony since they are gregarious and gang together in groups. It has several definite characteristics to help you in identification: the shell is solid, smooth, glossy and cylindrical in shape, like an olive, attaining a length of about two to three inches. It has a short spire and the outer lip is somewhat thickened. It is bluish gray, with a tracery of brownish and pink markings, which look like letters. It is found from North Carolina to Texas and also in the West Indies.

NETTED OLIVE *Oliva reticularis,* has a distinctive netlike pattern of purplish-brown lines covering the shell, which varies from white to brown. The shell is beautifully polished since the olive keeps its mantle protectively spread over its shell a good deal of the time and thus keeps it safe from damage. It is stouter and smaller than the lettered olive, only measuring about one and a half inches, but has the same contour. It is found primarily in southern Florida.

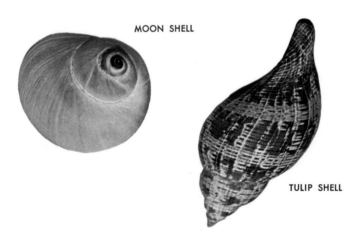

MOON SHELL

TULIP SHELL

34

PAINTED SNAILS

LETTERED OLIVE

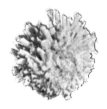

JEWEL BOX

FLAMINGO TONGUE

LEFT HANDED WHELK

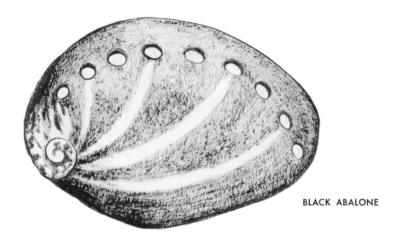

BLACK ABALONE

JEWEL BOX *Chama macerophylla* If you classify this shell by color, you won't be wrong since it is delicately toned in pink and rose to yellow. If you classify it by odd habits, you won't be wrong either since the valves are unequal in size and the larger one attaches itself firmly to rocks, coral growths or other shells, where it becomes so rigidly affixed that it is necessary to pry it loose with a hammer and chisel. The length is approximately three inches and it is found in deep water off the Florida coast.

FLAMINGO TONGUE *Cyphoma gibbosa* We shouldn't overlook white even though we are thinking of colors. The small but beautiful flamingo tongue proves this. The shell is long, narrow, about one inch in length, and glossy white or creamy white, with a raised ledge near the center. It is generally found attached to the sea-fan or some leafy aquatic plant. This capsule-looking snail is found from North Carolina to the West Indies.

ABALONE SHELLS are one of the most common and best-known shells on the Pacific Coast. The exterior is usually rough, hiding an iridescent, pearly lining. There is a series of holes near one margin of the shell, through which air is funneled since the abalone clamps itself tightly to a rock by means of its powerful suction foot. These openings serve an additional purpose since they help to keep the abalone in touch with its outside environment by sending out tentacle-like "feelers" through these holes.

BLACK ABALONE *Haliotis chacherodi,* has a smooth greenish black surface, concealing its silvery Christmas-toned green and red interior. The shell, which is up to 6 inches in length, has five to eight perforated holes, and is found from Oregon to southern California.

LEFT-HANDED WHELK or LIGHTNING CONCH *Busycon contrarium* Whelks come in a multitude of colors, shapes and sizes. The left-handed whelk (which is not a "freak" variety; the spire naturally turns to the left) is outstanding because of its size, which may average ten inches or more in height, and the grayish-white shell is strikingly marked with zigzag purplish-brown lines that give it the nickname "lightning conch."

## MARINE ODDITIES

On your shell collecting expeditions, you may encounter marine specimens which will add to the interest and appeal of your collection. If you are in the Gulf of Mexico area, you may be able to get a bit of velvet sponge or a rosette coral from one of the sponge divers. Other unusual marine varieties are:

### SEA URCHIN

These belong to the phylum *Echinodermata.* The sea urchin has a most unique covering, which is not strictly speaking a shell. Scientifically, it is called the "test." A test differs from a shell in the way it is made. The sea urchin test is composed of hard limestone plates produced by the inner tissues. Shells, on the other hand, are usually secretions from the outer tissues of a mollusk. Besides this unusual covering, the sea urchin is barbed with long, hinged spines, which perform the double task of protection and locomotion. Dead sea urchins lose these spines and what remains is a skeleton with rows of bumpy knobs that has often been compared to a pin cushion. These are highly fragile and are usually difficult to find complete. Another interesting feature is the fact that there is an opening in the middle of the lower surface, containing the mouth. Various species of sea urchins may be found on both the Atlantic and Pacific coasts.

COMMON SEA URCHIN *Arbacia punctulata,* is found on both coasts, but is a cold water species and its range on the eastern seaboard is north of Cape Cod; on the west coast it is from Washington northward. It has a test two to three inches in diameter, with one inch long spines. Although it is known as the Green Sea Urchin, which is the usual color, it may also be found with purplish and brownish tones. This is a close relative of the CALIFORNIA SEA URCHIN *Stronglocentratus franciscanus,* the most common variety in the California area. The EASTERN PURPLE SEA URCHIN *Arbacia punctulata* is found south of Cape Cod, on the Atlantic coast.

SAND DOLLAR

BASKET SEA STAR

## WESTERN LAMPSHELL

*Terebratalia occidentalis,* is a finely sculptured shell, which looks like the oil lamps used by the ancient Romans. It is found on the Pacific Coast, from Monterey, California, southward. Lampshells, although resembling mollusks, are in reality *Brachiopods.*

## SAND DOLLARS

If you see what looks like a silver dollar in the sand — look twice, it may be a sand dollar. The sand dollar is closely related to the sea urchin but its spines are not as fearsome since they are fine and silky-textured. Its test also differs from that of the sea urchin. It is in the form of a pancake disk, which looks like a silver dollar. It is found on the east coast from Maine to Florida, and on the west coast from Washington northward.

## BASKET SEA STAR

The starfish is one of the most familar and easily recognized marine animals. The jutting arms,which may be as few as five or as many as forty, give them their star-like form and have astonishing regenerative powers as new arms amazingly replace those that are broken or damaged.

BASKET SEA STAR *Astrophyton agassizi,* is basically shaped like the star fish but its flexible branching rays twist and turn into an incredible complex coiling network which forms a basket in which to trap its food. It is colored dull yellow or brown and grows as large as eight to twelve inches. It is one of the brittle star group, a deep-water form whose slender, fragile arms break off easily but speedily grow back.

SEA URCHINS                                                              M. Bacheller

## WHAT YOU WILL NEED TO GO SHELL COLLECTING

One of the many reasons why shell collecting is popular is the fact that you need a minimum of equipment and most of it you already have at home. Here is the basic equipment you will need:

1 — Rubber boots or sneakers

2 — Trowel or shovel for digging

3 — Strong pocket knife or spatula to pry loose specimens such as limpets or chitons; sometimes a hammer and chisel for stubborn species

4 — Small jars, such as medicine bottles, filled with sea water for tiny shells

5 — Waterproof or net bags, such as the bags in which oranges and grapefruit are often packed

6 — Enamel bucket filled with sea water. This is a convenience since some species, such as the Angel's Wing, will contract suddenly when taken from the water and break their shells

7 — Notebook and pencil to jot down data

As a precaution, do not mix large and small shells together. The smaller sizes can be easily damaged by the larger ones. In gathering live species, you've also got to be on guard since the larger mollusks sometimes eat the smaller ones.

Example of the wide variety of shells found on Sanibel and Captiva Islands, off the coast of Florida. From the author's collection, gathered by her two daughters.

ASTRAEA LONGISPINA

BERINGIUS KENNICOTTII

VELVET SPONGE

ROSETTE CORAL

## WHEN AND WHERE TO GO SHELL COLLECTING

The novice shell collector will begin with "dead" shells or those that have recently died. Shells collected on the beach have been battered by the waves, buffeted by the wind and bleached by the sun; bivalves are often split in half so that the shells are not always recognizable or worthwhile. As you grow more experienced, however, you will exercise more care and selectivity in your collection, and you will undoubtedly want the more attractive and the shinier specimens, which can only be gathered when the mollusk is alive.

Once you have graduated to the live stage of shell-collecting, you will want to know something about the best time to collect the live specimens.

Fortunately, many shell collectors say there is no such thing as a "best" time. The best time is when you have free time to go. But other conchologists prefer low tide. They claim that it is then that some species can be found, which may never be seen at any other time. Also at low tide many rocks are exposed.

But one of the great lures in hunting shells is the exciting anticipation of the unknown. A species of shell that is piled up on the beach one morning will have disappeared by eventide. Some shells appear seasonally, others appear only on rainy days. Storms may sweep in species that you might never ordinarily see. The best advice is to trust to luck, enjoy yourself, and hunt whenever you are able.

If there is no such thing as a "best" time, is there such a thing as a "best" place? Again half of the excitement lies in the fact that you can enjoy a wide latitude in hunting for shells and will sometimes discover them in the most unlikely places.

But here are some of the likely places where you can reasonably expect to find good specimens: tide pools, old docks, underneath wharves; under sand and on top of sand bars; under stones, in rock crevices; on seaweed and even on trees, close to the shoreline. A well-known conchologist says: "look everywhere" and that's just about the best advice.

## HOW TO CLEAN "LIVE" SHELLS

UNIVALVE SHELLS — Put in boiling water for one minute. Use a crochet hook or a hooked piece of wire to pull out the animal. You can also improvise a hook from a hairpin.

SMALL SPECIES OF UNIVALVE SHELLS — These may be too difficult to clean thoroughly with a hooked wire. Also, there is the danger that the shells can be damaged. For this reason, it is advisable to soak the shells in a four percent solution of formaldehyde for several days, then remove the body and dry the shell in the shade.

BIVALVES AND LARGE SPECIES OF UNIVALVES — Put in a basin of fresh water and bring slowly to a boil. Do not keep the shells in the hot water for more than a half hour. Remove the basin from the flame. By this time, the bivalve shells will have spread apart. As soon as the shells have cooled sufficiently to handle, remove the animal with a small paring knife.

TAPESTRY SHELL

STRIPED CONCH

LARGE SHELLS ENCRUSTED WITH BARNACLES AND MOSS — Dilute one table-spoonful of Clorox or a similar commercial cleaner in a quart of water. Use a glass or enamel container. Soak the shells for a few hours in the solution.

SHELLS WITH AN EPIDERMIS (PERIOSTRACUM) OR SKIN COVERING — Since the periostracum covers up the beauty and color of the shell, you may want to remove it. Prepare a solution of one pound of caustic soda to a gallon of water. Soak the shell for twenty-four hours. Remove with a tweezers as the solution is strong enough to burn your fingers.

FINAL "TOUCH-UP" — If you want to preserve your shells and enhance the color, go over them with a little mineral oil.

## HOW TO STORE YOUR SHELLS

You may start off simply with cigar boxes partitioned off into individual units or you may use large, sturdy cardboard containers for each class of mollusk, sectioning off the box for the individual species. You may exhibit your shells on book shelves or you may carefully set them up on cardboard trays in cabinets. The important thing is to work out a unified plan of organization. Small specimens may be kept in match boxes or in metal typewriter ribbon boxes.

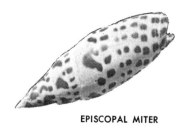

EPISCOPAL MITER

TOP SHELLS

PAINTED SHELLS                                                    M. Bacheller

## HOW TO LABEL YOUR SHELLS

Just as the card catalogue may be called the "heart" of the library so a precise catalogue of your specimens can be the scientific "heart" of your collection.

Each specimen should be numbered, beginning with number 1. Write the number directly on the shell with India ink or indelible ink. For odd-shaped shells, you may affix a small piece of adhesive tape on each shell, numbered in India ink.

This number should then be recorded on the label attached to the departmentalized box or tray in which the specimen is kept. It should also be marked down on the card index or in a loose-leaf notebook, in which you are going to keep your shell "diary."

A label should be as complete as possible. As a minimum, it should include the following: number; Latin name (Use the popular name at first, if in doubt, and fill in the Latin name after you have had time to check a field guide or at a museum); place where found, pinpointing the area as exactly as possible; the person by whom it was found. The loose-leaf notebook or card index will give all of the special enriching information, such as the details on the specimen: whether alive or dead; the condition of the beach; the tide; time of day; weather and other similar data.

# SHELL CRAFT

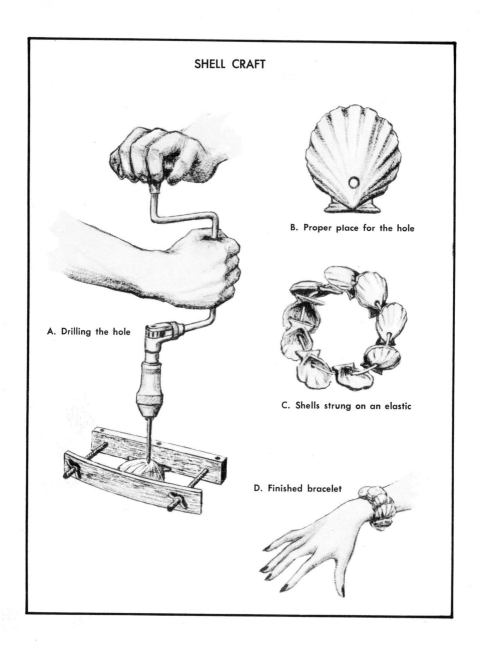

A. Drilling the hole

B. Proper place for the hole

C. Shells strung on an elastic

D. Finished bracelet

A sample label would look as follows:

SHELL COLLECTION OF IRVING CHERRY

BUSYCON PERVERSUM

DECEMBER 12, 1954

NO. 122

FOUND: ON THE BEACH AT CAPTIVA ISLAND, OFF THE COAST OF FLORIDA

BY: ANDREA CLAIRE

Shell collecting may start off casually. A day at the beach may result in a cache of shells which are too pretty to throw away. Visually, they are a delight. But shells that are merely pretty to look at, that are only used for shelf decoration, are just giving you half the enjoyment. It may be fun to pretend you hear the sound of the sea when you hold a conch shell to your ear but isn't it twice as interesting to know that those sounds are created by vibrations caused by air trapped inside the shell?

Science lends its own kind of magic to a hobby. Studying nature makes the world about you more exciting. The sea shell you hold in your hand may hold a world of wonders for you.

Various forms of marine life found in the sea wrack along the southern shore          B. Amlick

## THE SCIENCE-HOBBY SERIES

We specialize in publishing quality books for
young people. For a complete list please write

LERNER PUBLICATIONS COMPANY

241 First Avenue North, Minneapolis, Minnesota 55401